Refuge
the collected poetry of JJ Bola

Cover picture Kinshasa, Zaire (Democratic Republic of
Congo), circa 1991. Photographer unknown.

First published in the United Kingdom by:
OWN IT! Entertainment Ltd

Company Registration Number: 09154978

Copyright © 2018 JJ Bola
JJ Bola has asserted his right under the Copyright, Designs and
Patents Act 1988 to be identified as the author of this work.

ISBN: 9780-995458994

WWW.OWNIT.LONDON

"JJ Bola's poems are packed full of beauty, awe, hope and intimacy. They are, above all, prayers to love and life. Let them lift you up and blow you gently away."
- Poetry and Words, Glastonbury Festival

"Totally blown away by the poetry of @JJ_Bola at the @frankieboyle gig tonight!Go see him! Buy his book!"
- @lucyjlowe on Twitter

"First time I realised that I didn't actually hate poetry was hearing JJ Bola at the end sexual violence in war summit."
- @LK_Pennington on Twitter

"If you haven't read @JJ_Bola's poetry yet, GET ON IT."
- @MaameBlueWrites on Twitter

"Saw @JJ_Bola lastnight at the Lincoln University night of enrichment so amazing, currently obsessed with his poetry."
- @Wallace_x_ on Twitter

"Powerful poetry from @JJ_Bola. If you aren't following him already, please, rectify that. He's rather brilliant."
- @angelwhispers_ on Twittter

"Whether in the audience watching him perform or reading by yourself, JJ Bola's poetry will hit you, force you to think and make you feel alive."
- Consented UK

poems

poems

refuge

noun:
the state of being safe or sheltered
from pursuit, danger, or difficulty.
a place or situation providing safety or shelter.

synonyms:
shelter, protection, safety, security, asylum, sanctuary; poetry

the key

she wears a cage around her heart.
and there aren't many brothers, lovers, or others
that she would let come close enough to pull apart those bars
she says, 'i need to, it's for protection.'
too many times has she been hurt before.
felt the swiftness of the sword slice through her dreams
like samurais on the front line of a war
'why does love have to feel like a battle field?' she asks
'...when nothing's worth fighting for.'
so i wonder, who sees the visions of the blind?
who hears the prayers of the deaf?
even the mute agrees that some things are better left unsaid.
all things. so, she stays silent and hides behind her smile.
a smile so bright that it reminds even those contemplating suicide
that life is still worth living. but beneath that smile her soul
starts to grimace. she sits unforgiving and watches the world go by
her window, listening to echoes of her past life, burning effigies
in her mind of a love she couldn't find
'it could all be so simple
but you had to make it hard.'
she still carries the scars.
stab wounds set tracks across her back like warrior marks
'i am a warrior!'
there are no feelings inside. oceans, seas, and rivers has she cried
she would pull the sun out of the sky just to show you how dark
her days, she has no name. hell fire, sulphur, and brimstone
can't tame her rage but still she cries. she would never
admit it though, but all you would have to do is ask her pillow.

'why should I love? what has love ever done for me?
i used to sing, paint and write poetry,
and all i ever wanted was for someone to love me for me.'
she spoke, with a croak in her voice as if her throat had swelled
from all the lies she'd been fed.

her stomach is a cemetery, a burial ground for the butterflies
she used to get. i sat quietly listening and then replied
'how can you expect to love, when you hold your heart in a cage
and won't let it be free?

you're searching for a man who's strong enough to pull apart
those bars, but you're the one who holds the key.'

let love set you free.

an apology

to all the sisters everywhere, i'm sorry.
i'm sorry for what commercial rap and hip-hop music videos
did to you. they removed the very essence that made you beautiful:
your spirit.
your intelligence.
your strength.
your minds were revered and illuminous
like fire flies in the night sky
but it has been replaced with an image of degradation.
a masterpiece smeared, humiliation, a miseducation that is passed
on to daughters, and daughters of daughters
given the wrong lessons to learn, not knowing their true selves.

and now when lost brothers run around
trying to block out your shine
remember no one can take away your glow that lies inside.
but if you just let me borrow that glow, i will multiply and place it
behind every dark cloud that looms over a lost brother
or a motherless child
because the golden lining is your presence in our lives.
the very thing that gives us hope when we are down.
and i want to chase the voice of the truth of your words
with a butterfly net, catch it and then set it free into classrooms
so, the lessons that little boys will receive is to understand you.
and when they grow up to be men
they will know how to treat you.

on my lonely nights when i thirst for love
and i wish i could be first for love but my fountain has run dry
i want to go swimming in your waters.
and i pray that it is these same waters that fill the oceans,
rivers and seas
and rains down on us from the skies
with little droplets of forgiveness

to wash away our transgressions, because i am truly sorry.
i'm sorry for the derogatory epithets and the slanderous names
because we are not brave enough to rise up with you
so, we try to bring you back down low, calling you
'bitches' and 'hoes'
and i wish i could catch the breath of anyone who ever dared
to say it to you again. i would rip that breath from their chest
and place it underneath the wings of the sankofa bird
that flies across the jet-black sky speaking of your beauty.
and when that bird returns
i would take back that breath, place it back in their chest
so those who once spoke ill of you,
would know how to address you best
and call you sister, or queen. or just by your name.
either way. i'm sorry.

i'm sorry for those of us, who didn't consider the effects
of leaving behind a child to be raised with no father figure.
and giving you the impossible burden
of being a mother and a father
at the same time. the truth is, no man could ever fill the shoes
of a mother, no matter how hard he tries.
but you, you did so gloriously rise to the occasion
and tip toed across the hot coals of single parenthood
overcoming many obstacles and situations.
i'm sorry for all the hard times.

i'm sorry for all the lies
that come from those of us who can't handle
commitment and are scared, we turn away from your light because
we can't handle the glare
and then we wonder why the darkness is still there
are we blind? we can't see the truth from the lies,
so instead we use our eyes to lust. and pierce
the holistic image of God's design. You.
you are divine.

i want to take that divinity
and inject it into the mitochondrial cells of your DNA
so you would only give birth to angels.
those angels would carry war torn cities on their backs
and fly them away to a day
where the sound of gunshots are replaced
by the echoes of children's laughter.
those same angels would lift the spirits of abandoned nations
to the highest heights,
where the visions of former martyrs are realised
visions of peace, visions of prosperity, visions of unity.
i'm sorry because sometimes it seems like we do not even try.
i'm sorry for all the pain that we have brought into your lives
and if i could, i would catch each tear that fell from your eyes
and transform them into diamonds.
then i would sprinkle those diamonds across the night sky to form
a new constellation, and i would wish upon a star that one day
we could be
as divine as you are.

shooting stars

a star exploded in the midst of her breath
bringing new life
as we sat paying homage to the night
constellations were tattooed across the front of her chest.
i traced her lineage to find that she was born of a star
and when she spoke each one came back to her.
i ran my fingers through her mind
caressed each alphabet blind and read her thoughts.
she said she'd been taught to mask the tragedy in her skin.
that invisibility was now a gift so that her pain could not be seen.
in between each breath she maintained
that even shooting stars lose their way
and as one went by i said 'look at the night sky,
how can anyone ever dare to say that it is no longer beautiful?'

politics 101

what kind of world are we living in?
where fat cats get paid dividends
on investments they made
lying cheating and stealing.
and at the bottom you've got kids
as drug dealers but at the top
pharmaceutical companies make millions
selling drugs, manipulating disease and illnesses.

i once heard someone say
if you're rich you get to live.
our state of mind is poor
like we've got nothing left to give.
it's like we're stuck in the wilderness
cannibalistic tendencies living like savages
in an environment so primitive a knowledge
so limited because we still can't figure out
how they built the pyramids
but we call this civilisation.

we have nations who order
the torture and slaughter
of innocent lives across the water.
perpetrating lies without purpose.
perpetuating lies in a media circus.
this is modern day colonisation.
a symbiotic invasion. an occupation
by nations causing chaos and disorder.
globalisation is their vision.
enforcing the laws of capitalism
across all foreign lands.
wage war. strategy four. reward those
who conform to their system. and silence

the voices of those who oppose or won't listen.
but the cataclysm's got our tongue
so, we stay silent. just sit back and watch
but even the hands on a broken clock
are right twice a day so when they tell us
what time it is we accept what they say.
remember when they said its time for change?

well what's changed?
it's just a change of face on the same game.
presenting the same claim.
inflicting the same pain.
collecting the same gain.
they wreak havoc for the black gold.
it doesn't matter
how many lives they have to take.
how many homes they have to break.
how many enemies they create.
it's for the oil's sake.
because oil translates
into capital.
so, they move in on capitals.
just so they can cap it all.
this is politics 101 with a capital P.
first lesson is:
don't trust what you read in the news
or what you see on TV.

i just wanna love her

i just wanna love her
like a mother loves a new born child
because she makes me feel like i'm running wild
among the stars above,
as i look down on the earth
whilst strolling across the floor of the universe
i realise i wanna love her because i recognize her worth.
have you ever woken up in the morning?
thinking about the exact same thing
that you thought about the night before?
and wondered whether or not you even slept
because you woke up in the exact same position
you were lying from? i just wanna love her
but i find myself having to hold back my right hand
with my left hand because so much of the time
 it's her phone number that my thumb quickly finds.
and i have to try so hard just so i don't text her
every five minutes, like 'hi, what you up 2?', 'lol, lol.'
even when she's not in the country
i wanna talk to her for hours,
i don't care what the tariff will cost me
but thank goodness for Skype.

i just wanna love her 'cos she's exactly my type
and sometimes i find myself logging on to Facebook
just to stare at her picture.
such fine form
she's got the kind of smile that will make you feel re-born.
the other day
i was walking down the road
i threw my hands in the air and screamed out 'yes!'
just because I know her,
and i'm getting all these mixed feelings

because i've got so much love to show her.
she's got me confused; do i stay or do i go
do we take it fast or slow
buy a flat or a home,
and we're not even there yet.
i just wanna love her like the moon loves the sea,
like the birds and the bees,
like the sun to the trees.
and just like the trees to the sun
i would reach up to wherever she was
so we could touch and be one.

i just wanna love her because her roots run deep.
when she speaks, she doesn't know it
but she has the same grace as ancient Queens.
she has the wisdom of Tiye
and the beauty of Nefertiti,
she's fierce like Nzinga,
and a courageous leader like the Queen of the Ashanti.
and because i'm a King
i know that together we'll rule with love.
the same love that makes angels sing
as they look down on us from above.
and if i could meet the angel that put together
the plan that her and i should meet
and had the courage to suggest it to God,
i would kneel down and shake her hand
because it was an idea of pure genius.
and i can just imagine God's reactions like
'yeah, I'm definitely feeling this.'
but God already knew that this was going to happen
between her and me,
because it was written by Her hand in the book of destiny.

i just wanna love her
like she's already my wife

and together, we've started a brand-new life.
and just to prove how much i love her,
i would make the same sacrifice as Christ
and come back to life, so i could be with her for the rest of her
days.
if you were to cut me, i would probably bleed love
because I can feel it running through my veins.
i'm sure my blood type is L-O-V-E positive
though my doctor doesn't seem to agree with this.

i just wanna love her so much
she's got me talking to my pastor,
and i'm telling him that its love i wanna master,
as if it's a form of fine art.
in a sense i guess it is
because together, i know that her and i would create
a masterpiece that would make the chapel of Sistine
look like it was made by children in primary. school
is not a place where you can learn of love like this.
sometimes i just wanna lay my head down
and fall asleep on her pillow lips. you know them days
when nothing pays, and nothing seems to go your way
i just wanna love her
because she makes me feel like together, we could ride
any wave, and just sail away, on our relation – ship
in search of a brighter day. then i look at her hips
and i see the future, the next generation. the dream
of holding our first-born child, fills my heart with elation
it's our legacy that i'm contemplating.

i just wanna love her like each day is the last
and if i come to find,
that tomorrow brings the end of my time
i hope i'll die her best friend. another thing i hope for
is that i would have met her by then.

london

listen as she breathes,
this city.
it makes promises in the form of dreams
and keeps them in places that are hard to see.
on street corners and pavement slopes
pockets full of hope. a kaleidoscope of emotions
trickle
down
the gutter.
a rainbow appears
it's raining,
but that is not new here.
it rains fears and regret.
nights out we'd rather forget.
sweat, swept from nervous foreheads
where secrets are better kept
secret.
here, lies spread like wild fire
but what of truth, what truth do we speak of?
we keep our upper lip stiff. nobody listens.
think quick, people shine, but their minds
don't glisten, so fifteen minutes
isn't a long enough time, but we each want our
claim to fame. the smoke covers the window panes
and mirrors, so we don't see ourselves clearly.
our reflection is but a memory.
a fading image of what we once used to be,
lovers,
livers of life,
before we gave it up for the mundane.
but do you remember the days
when we'd reach the top of the climbing frame
and feel like we'd just conquered Everest?

the days when we could speak our hearts,
without being drunk on beverages?
the days when we believed,
in ourselves,
in each other?
the city lights sparkle,
like a beautiful woman's eyes,
London always leaves me breathless.
there is a peace that slips through my fingers
and gets buried in the ground.
one day, when love will pour down
i hope we would have all found
what we've been looking for.

if you cut (we all bleed) London, 2011

when a child is not initiated into the village,
it will burn it down just to feel its warmth.

you abort the dreams of young teens
so now many of them can't see a future.
and many of them won't.
still, you plant your seed of infertile indoctrination
into their minds so they don't ever grow.
everything stays the same, so a change never shows.

to you, 'change' is just a political sound bite to win you votes.
to them, it was a symbol of hope.
but then you tightened the rope
and opened your Pandora's Box of policies
unleashing budget cuts and high tuition fees
in these times of austerity,
tell me how can you still find the money
to fund war in other countries?
did you hear the young man speak when he said
'you cannot stretch your hands, to where your arms cannot reach?'
before you walk away from the murder scene,
tell me how many dreams have you already looted internationally?

lawlessness creates lawlessness.

so, what is it about this society that can breed
such mindless violence and criminality?
we've replaced role models with celebrity, beautiful withsexy,
generosity with greed, we do not know the difference between
what we want and what we need. what happened to community?

if you cut, we all bleed.

what is it about this society that can breed such criminality?
protesting was for a righteous cause, against wars, fighting for
human rights and equality, but now rioting and looting happens
for laptops, iPhones and BlackBerrys, Nike Air trainers from JD

if you cut, we all bleed.

materialism is infectious like a disease,
children are seen as just a marketing strategy.
research the companies,
capitalism is the biggest looter of them all.
it has taken away more businesses and homes.
another illusion and a fallacy
just like the lies that were told by the police.
a mother cries. the sad thing is after all of this
is said and done, and we return to normality
a mother will still be crying.
how many mothers have cried?
how many more mothers need to cry?
stop the violence, stop the lies.
nobody needs to suffer in silence.
stop taking away the peace from people's lives.

if you cut, we all bleed.

such greed. now families are left without a home.
many left alone, on the streets to roam.
what is it about society that can breed such criminality?
because children do not raise themselves
and apples do not fall far from the tree.
there is a collective responsibility
because everybody is hurting, i can feel your frustration.
but in spite of the pain
do not look for someone to blame.
because remember that when you point the finger
remember

it's often in the direction that you need to go.
collective responsibility.

if you cut, we all bleed.
do not amputate your own future.

real men

i was told to be a man, a real man.
apparently, that meant never to cry.
that meant my eyes had to be like shutters,
so, when it came to feelings
my emotions were like a church monastery; i had none.

i was told that to cry was to show weakness
but in this world, you have to be strong to survive.
walk with a mask on your face, a screw face
and never show what's going on inside.
from young, we were taught how to make guns
out of fingers, until we were old enough to shoot them.
guard your heart from the start, we danced
bad, to Michael Jackson, thrill(h)er, until we became
real life smooth criminals. conditioned by the subliminal
it isn't our human nature, it is indoctrination.
our voices were silenced so we practised violence on all platforms
from Play Station and Xbox to that boy Michael's face.
we were never taught it was wrong, because as a real man
anger is the only conditioned accepted response.
just think of how uncomfortable you get
when you see a grown man cry. think of the times
when your mother said 'wipe your tears, big boys don't cry.'
so, it's no surprise to see that in society, men commit up to 90%
of all violent crimes because we are always angry inside.
so, to be a real man, is to live a lie.

i was told to be a real man
so misogynistic words like 'bitches,' lingered in the tip bits
of our tongues. we lived in concrete blocks with no gardens
but would still ask, 'where the hoes at?'
listen bro, the fact is we were lied to.
we were told that it's okay for a man

to sleep with as many women as he wants,
but we were never told about love.
never told that love could heal the greatest pain
like a needle to the vain, it is the drug that we need.
i wish we could sell bags of love
instead of crack and weed,
just imagine the change you would see.
crack addicts would just be people, who were high on love.
crack babies would just be babies, who were born with love.
and rehab would be where all the haters went.
the fact is we were lied to. given negative images to aspire to.
so, to be a real man is just another lie too.

this goes out, to all the men
who are real, because they have beating hearts.
who aren't afraid to cry.
men whose emotions show as clear as the moonlit sky.
men who write poetry in the middle of the night and read books.
and meet up at the coffee shop or library to discuss
bell hooks – We Real Cool.
men who can say I love you or give each other hugs without saying
'no homo.'
men,
who can speak of love openly.
like an envelope, open me and you will see what is written inside.
men who want love, but not that kind you make in the club
the kind that your ancestors once spoke of. it isn't a myth.
imagine 'Roses are Red' written in hieroglyphs. Ode
To A Naked Beauty in Meroitic script. Swahili spoken word
across the Serengeti, about how the sunrise over the horizon,
reminds us of the beauty in a woman's face when she smiles.

listen bro, the fact is we were lied to.
given negative images for us to aspire to
so why would you want to be a real man,
when you can be you?

so be you.
do not be confined by society's ideals
because real men don't exist,
only men who are real.

live

people should smile more, for no reason.
should appreciate life more, in any season.
and in any season
people should know how to dress appropriately.
we see way too many half naked bodies
when it's average temperature with just a little bit of sunshine.
people should feel free to say whatever's on their minds,
and not keep it all inside.
people should support each other during the hardest times
and not be afraid to reach out. compassion isn't a crime
at least not for now.

people should take days off work more often
and spend them watching the clouds
and looking up at the sky,
wondering how and why we came to be.
people should chase their dreams.
life is never quite what it seems. failure
if taken as a lesson, is the pathway to success
so, keep on chasing until you reach your last breath.
make sure you live with no regrets, they eat away at your soul.
so, go and find that long lost friend that you fell out with for no
reason.
exercise so you feel healthy; get in shape but
not in a narcissistic way. your heart is alive. feel it beat against
your chest. let the adrenaline flow through your veins
as your feet explores the earth a thousand times over.
run that marathon you intended, for that charity you like.
the one that stirs your emotions and brings old memories
back to life. like when my basketball coach died of cancer
i remember that night i cried. tell someone you love them,
before it's too late. call your mother and tell her thank you.
look to the person sitting beside you, and just say 'hi'.

people should read more poetry. and support the artists
by buying their material. seriously
people should take themselves less seriously.
honestly, there's nothing wrong with dancing and singing out loud
on the underground, people should talk to each other
where is it written that we shouldn't? and why is it always
on the underground, that you see the one person
that you would really like to talk to but never on the bus.
people should walk slowly, i know you find it annoying
but you notice so much more. when was the last time
you opened your front door to a stranger?
why are we so scared of everything?
who watches the watchmen?
and who watches the watchmen, watching the watchmen?
and in the end, who's watching them?
i don't watch men, i'm just not that way inclined
but people should learn to tolerate
and let other people get on with their lives.
people should make the most of their time.
live. people should live.
in the moment. for all we have is the present.
tomorrow may never come. and if it doesn't, make today
the day that you wrote your name into the stars
shining brightly along your journey wherever you may be.

daughter of the sun

summer's day at night.
the beautifully synchronised
dance of two butterflies
carried by the breeze on to a flower.
the song of the early bird,
the wave of a river
11th hour, life giver
come nearer and breathe into me.
lungs polluted. soul commuted
in search across the seas and returned
only to find you here. i burned
candle-tip tongue speaking too long
of a flame that came once and was gone
forever.

come nearer, speaker of truth
realising that i had never loved
before i met you.
in search of proof of divine
i close my eyes only to find
your visage outlined.
teacher of deities; I and I is now we.
come nearer and speak to me.
let sacred lips part like Red Sea
revealing true path away from old torture.

daughter of the sun

blades of grass worship you
moonlight cascades onto your skin.
glow firefly, darkness yielding.
stretched wings across horizons
cities whisper your name.

come nearer and whisper your name to cities
with buildings as tall as dreams.
a thousand stories for a generation
growing with hope. let all your fears go
and come to me.

to her, where she may be

you are an enigma, a mystery.
the aurora borealis of my darkened skies,
the child like imagination of my adult mind.

you are the moon's harmony
composed in the key of tranquility.
a concerto of nine violins played by
the ten suns of Di Jun,
you are the tears of the last son that shines.

you are the in between of time.
the days and nights of Brahma.
timeless like Kalpas,
you give me vibrations
like the beating of Djembe drums.

you are every creation story ever penned.
an epic with no words.
your words have grown wings
and flown from the page.

your story is now in the air

and in my blindness
i capture your words in brail
for those moments when i can't see you
i'll still be able to feel what you say.

faith

on my lonely days i breathe night
'til the stars permeate my lungs
so, from my veins i bleed light.
i touch both ends of my darkness
then pierce my side
and let the constellations pour onto the floor
so you could find your path to mine.

my sacrifice. i have loved you in spirit
written your lyrics on my pupils
so my eyes could study your lesson; your image.
your message i engraved onto waves of tranquility
searching for inner peace in a piece of me
so the finger-tips of my tongue could taste the essence
that is written on your lips.
i kissed
you into existence.
held you somewhere in the distance
between dreams and sleep
neither hell nor purgatory could keep me
from the heavens of your touch.
i've known too much,
only to come to know that i do not know enough.

so if ever the cold hand of this world
plucks the feathers
from our wings and renders us grounded
if the air of this planet pollutes our hopes
until only by our fears we are surrounded
if the ground we walk on crumbles
until our paths are erased,
i will be there for the rest of your days.
for this world,

this world has too sudden
become a place for those who despise divinity,
but i see the god in you
and it gives me faith
so, still, i close my eyes and i pray.

moon child

life is the complex amalgamation
of the beautiful and tragic. the beautiful is she,
the tragic is knowing that i will never be with her.
never feel the smooth of her skin, the soft of her hair
place my hands on the small of her back or hold them
together like a prayer. we pray for love
but we say love is blind so it's no surprise
that it rarely finds, its way to us. we stood worlds apart
but then you moved closer and smiled it reminded me
of my childhood; all that was joy and laughter. playing
runouts, hopscotch and had, cassette tapes and pencils, dancing
to Michael Jackson Bad, real bad. i dreamed a stencil
of your silhouette outlined in the moon.
Moon Child,
your glow was too bright for my eyes
made dull by the sorrows of this world.

i watched you walk by
like a ballerina on a cloud, like notes on a hymn sheet
you were a beautiful harmony. i imagined your voice
like peace to a nation at war. your face
brought a stillness to my heart that is only matched with poetry.
but as you moved closer to me
i felt the blood rush through my veins
like a thousand stampeding elephants.

broken blissful benevolence

excuse me for my silence
i was simply in awe.
last i saw was you walk out of the door
knowing that i was never going to see you again
i decided to write this poem to remind me

that in each day life gives us the opportunity
to turn something from the tragic into the beautiful.
so i'll say these words
and hope that they are carried up by the wind
like candle lit lanterns across the night sky
so if you ever see them, these words, burning bright
know that they were for you.

prodigal son

return like the prodigal son. word to the one
your beauty deserves homage like the glow of the sun.
from the stars to the moon, the highest point in the noon
we'll pave a way never delay for our journey is true.
this is spiritual. in every sense a higher virtue.
no need for rituals for love alone dictates what we do.

close my eyelids
reminisce on nights searching for Isis. Osiris
the god i was but now just blinded. reminded
of better days living through the darkest haze
looking for hope. fighting fears.
waiting for the light of brighter days
that exists within us. and goes on without doubt.
what do you do when you're trapped in but feel left out?
when you're giving minimum but feel maxed out?
sometimes you need to question what life is about?

and when you're running
but you only run from yourself.
this world's view of heaven is kind of like my hell.
i still see things that make my heart swell.
we've all got a story to tell so i stand to the side
shared my vision with the blind, sang a song with the deaf.
made sure i move right so i stepped to the left.

now i walk with each step
on the road less travelled, mysteries unraveled
i was picking up boulders like it was gravel.
on journey through space and time
looked up realised that His face was mine
He said *take your time. soon you will find and the day will come.*
you can't know where you're going unless you know where you're from.

i found hip hop

i found hip hop lying in a comatose state
on a cassette tape labelled 1998.
so i put it in the radio and pressed play
and the first place i heard hip hop
was in my mother's voice.
the weight of her pain was too heavy
for her words to explain but i could see it written
clearly across her face.

i kept looking. and i found hip hop.
an ancient tradition now sold out by capitalism so
the only return we get on an investment is cash money
50 cent and 2 chains. i found hip hop. on a runaway slave
with two chains. one around his feet the other around his
brain. so, go figure
and excuse me that i still feel the pain
if someone calls me and says *that's my n...*
because on them ships they used to say *that's my n...*
think quicker. history is bigger than slavery and colonisation.
i am African; we are one people from many nations.

i found hip hop. in the struggle. in the Haitian rubble
and the Congo mist. Olympic podium clenched fist. the war cry
of Toussaint L'Ouverture and Dessalines. the poetry
of Patrice Lumumba's Independence Day speech. and the flow
of a Thomas Sankara freestyle on the roads of Burkina Faso.
but now brothers on the corner getting lean. leech on the blood
that flows in the veins of a crack fiend trying to forget the pain.
the day a pregnant teen makes her way to the abortion clinic
turning her womb into a tomb. her cervix into a cemetery.
too soon. more warriors we lose. the truth we choose
to confuse from the lies.

i found hip hop. on the estates.
scriptures scratched inside dodgy lifts. broken gates.
graffiti etched on walls like hieroglyphs. grandmother
carrying the family's shopping up the stairs on a rainy day.
started from the bottom means nothing
if your people are still there. what is even hip hop now anyway?

hip is the knowledge.
like the construction of the pyramids.
spiritual mathematics. the Ishango bone
of the Bantu Kongo.

hip is the knowledge.
like the school kid
who gets sent out of class
because they ask challenging questions.

hip is the education
that we never receive from the mainstream institutions.

hop is the movement.
like Gil Scott Heron; *the revolution will not be televised.*
hop is the movement.
like Marcus Garvey had 6 million followers worldwide.
hop is the movement.
hear the footsteps of sisters
who lead the revolution;
Yaa Asantewa. Kimpa Vita.
and Nanny of the Maroons.
if we're not careful
they'll do to hip hop
just like they did jazz and blues.
you'll recognise the sound but you won't
know its roots.
so, to hip hop you've got to stay true.
hip hop is the knowledge and movement.

hip hop is you.

i'm talking about *hip hop* so don't act *Like You Never*
heard *The Thieves Banquet* Kill the Radio. *The People* know.
it's *Common Sense* that *There Is A Light*. a *Black Star*
that shines *Below the Heavens*. we've got the *Blueprint*
to the constellations. *Brand Nubians* on astral navigation
across the skies. *Black on Both Sides* of the universe. *Jeanius*
is the gift and the curse of humanity. in *My Country*
i'm out for presidents to represent me (say what?!).
i'm out for presidents to represent me.
i'm out for presidents to represent me.
i'm out for dead presidents to represent me...

i didn't find hip hop. hip hop found me.

refuge

imagine how it feels to be chased out of home.
to have your grip ripped. loosened from your
fingertips, something you so dearly held on to.
like a lover's hand that slips when pulled away
you are always reaching.

my father would speak of home. reaching.
speaking of familiar faces. girl next door
who would eventually grow up to be my mother.
the fruit seller at the market. the lonely man
at the top of the road who nobody spoke to.
and our house at the bottom of the street
lit up by a single flickering lamp
where beyond was only darkness. there
they would sit and tell stories
of monsters that lurked and came only at night
to catch the children who sat and listened to
stories of monsters that lurked.
this is how they lived. each memory buried.
an artefact left to be discovered by archaeologists.
the last words on a dying family member's lips. this
was sacred. not even monsters could taint it.
but there were monsters that came during the day.
monsters that tore families apart with their giant hands.
and fingers that slept on triggers. the sound of gunshots
ripping through the sky became familiar like the tapping
of rain fall on a window sill. monsters that would kill
and hide behind speeches, suits and ties. monsters
that would chase families away forcing them to leave
everything behind. i remember
when we first stepped off the plane.
everything was foreign. unfamiliar. uninviting.
even the air in my lungs left me short of breath.

we came here to find refuge. they called us refugees
so, we hid ourselves in their language
until we sounded just like them.
changed the way we dressed to look just like them.
made this our home until we lived just like them
and began to speak of familiar faces. girl next door
who would grow up to be a mother. the fruit seller
at the market. the lonely man at the top of the road
who nobody spoke to. and our house
at the bottom of the street lit up by a flickering lamp
to keep away the darkness. there
we would sit and watch police that lurked
and came only at night to arrest the youths who sat
and watched police that lurked and came only at night.
this is how we lived.

i remember one day i heard them say to me
they come here to take our jobs
they need to go back to where they came from
not knowing that i was one of the ones who came.
i told them that a refugee is simply
someone who is trying to make a home.
so next time when you go home
tuck your children in and kiss your families
goodnight, be glad that the monsters
never came for you.
in their suits and ties.
never came for you.
in the newspapers with the media lies.
never came for you.
that you are not despised.

and know that deep inside
the hearts of each and every one of us
we are all always reaching
for a place that we can call *home.*

this is not just

another war.
not just another group of rebels fighting
without a cause. puppets on a string. stealing
riches from a nation's poor.
people suffering. this is not just
another fight.
not another plight of a people
as the screams of teenagers echo into the night.

we've turned pages in history.
gone from dark ages into the light
but this is not just
another struggle that we will one day
leave behind.

not just
another thought on the back
of our minds as long it doesn't interrupt
with our lives, we choose
only that which our conscience can bare. we lose
our humanity
every time we stare at a television.
every time we eat in McDonalds.
sat by the window seat of a Starbucks
with a cappuccino reading the latest pop book.
every time we download an app
on our iPhone. iPad. i am alone.

this is not just
what happens here to the little girl
broken to pieces hiding her tears.
never allow your fears
to be greater than your dreams.
i rarely cry but every time i write

i shed streams. this is not just poetry.
this is a prayer. this is eyes closed
bended knees hands together in the air.
this is for every struggle in humanity.
from the Middle East to east Congo
we are not alone.

this is not just for me.
this is for the homeless person
begging on the streets.
this is for the single mother.
the clinically depressed.
the war child: post-traumatic stress disorder.
the daughter of a rape victim.
this is for the ones who cry.
and for the ones who hold it all in.
the beautiful ones who are not yet born.
this is for the ones
who struggle their whole lives
and will only know scorn.
this is to humanity.
this is not just.

99

they say this is for our freedom
yet they kill for peace. they hate for love.
fill our lives with lies. indoctrination so
we now despise everything including the truth
though we barely recognise what it is.
we no longer dare to live. instead we hide.
behind screens. online. out of sight. we intellectually
verbalise premature ejaculation how can this be pro-creation?
when we abortion everything including our dreams.

somebody please tell me what it means
when it seems you're the last one who really cares?
so many hollow eyes that stare back at you, souls drifting
into the sea, sinking in the depth. i would dare
to give my next breath if it would be the seed
that would grow the tree of life, so we could live again.
but i cannot make that sacrifice. i am not Horus. Krishna. Christ.
i cannot Atlas this world onto my shoulders
when finger tips on revolvers are the decision makers.
when the lease of life is held upon a holster and fate is decided
by the distance between the hand to the hip.
sometimes the best i can do is cry.

so i cry.
for the 99 times whips cracked on backs
and rubber bullets. triggers and the 99 fingers that pull it.
for the 99 families that mourn with every sunrise.
and the 99 women just raped in an eastern Congo village.
the blood and oil spillage. for the 99 miles of coastline
destroyed by nuclear waste. and the 99 times
we were promised a change that never came. i cry.
these tears are my cocoon and every 99 days
i am reborn trying to find the balance between the heavy
and the light but the weight weighs down on me,

so i wait for a way to weigh these ways so i can wei-wu-wei
philosophically back to where i need to be. into the ether.
for this world isn't mine. i barely recognise what it's become.
what will i do when that day comes
when my first-born son will look at me and say
dad, *what happened to humanity?*
with my nervous hands and trembling tongue
before my heart finds its feet and jumps out of my chest
i'll put down my cape and remove the superman complex
that seems to come with fatherhood.
then i can only hold my breath and hope to find the words
that will deflect the pain that he will feel when he realises
that this world was stolen from him too.
after all what can I say?
Son...

where we wait for god

a thousand hands clamped together
like scaffolding, holding up a building
of prayers.
where inside lives dreams of children growing.
flowing like water. streams of hope for pencils
in hands before guns. of fields of flowers. daffodils
and dandelions, before land mines. bombs stepped on
limbs torn apart like trust in a family feud.

of market sellers. women with blues
written on their skin. the food they sell is faith
for the futures of their daughters. that they may
understand their fate is more than just to marry
their husbands or to be raped by rebels or soldiers.

we wait for God.
with Jesus perched on the edge of lips
hanging at the end of every sentence
like lynched black bodies from a tree
or the smile of a new born child.
this bittersweet, damning salvation
this imprisoning liberation, this despair
hope
to be free.
we
wait beneath clouds; rain falls down like bullets
in the east. little boys with empty stomachs in mines
digging for currency. money does not grow on trees
it grows in the ground but it is
always someone else
who eats
always someone else
who feasts

always someone else
with peace.

we speak of this war but the cries fall
on deaf ears so we wait for a god with ears
like ripe soil so we can plant these prayers
and watch them grow. but we are still waiting
a thousand hands clamped together
holding up a country.

a different violence

it is one thing to be killed. left
for hours on cold concrete.
choked until your black is blue. beat
to a pulp. chalk outlined from
6 shots. 9 shots. even shots whilst you sleep.
rough rope on smooth of skin. hanging.

but to have to change your voice.
the way you speak. to talk like *this*.
to always have your hands shown.
to wear your hair any way but how it grows.
to leave *yourself* at home. and wear that
smile. that suit. shirt and tie. because it makes you look less
you. to shrink. to change the way you think.
to publicly apologise for that crime
you had no involvement in. to remind
them that you are not like *them*.
to have to fit in.
this is a different kind of violence.

tell them (they have names)

and when they turn the bodies over
to count the number of closed eyes.
and they tell you 800'000: you say
no. that was my uncle. he wore bright
coloured shirts and pointy shoes.

2 million: you say no. that was my aunty.
her laughter could sweep you up like
the wind to leaves on the ground.

6 million: you say no. that was my mother.
her arms. the only place i have ever
not known fear.

3 million: you say no. that was my love.
we used to dance. oh, how we used to dance.
or 147: you say no. that was our hope. our future.
the brains of the family.

and when they tell you
that you come from war: you say
no. i come from hands held in prayer
before we eat together.

when they tell you that you
come from conflict: you say
no. i come from sweat. on skin.
glistening. from shining sun.

when they tell you
that you come from genocide: you say no.
i come from the first smile of a new born child.
tiny hands.

when they tell you
that you come from rape: you say
no. and you tell them about every time
you have ever loved.

tell them that you are from mother
carrying you on her back.
until you could walk. until you could run.
until you could fly.

tell them that you are from father
holding you up to the night sky. full of stars.
and saying look, child. this is what you are made of.
from long summers. full moons.
flowing rivers. sand dunes.
you tell them that you are an ocean
that no cup could ever hold.

a heavy weightless thing

it comes slowly and silently. with autumn cloud tenderness. warm handed it will hold you caress and lull you softly into its sleep. or it comes all together at once. loud and sudden. like thunder. violent like a fist that hits whilst you are looking the other way. whilst you are dreaming. of tomorrow. it will grab the future from your vision until you can see only today.it is heavy. like the heaviest weightless thing you have ever carried. the burden of it will not fall upon your hands and shake it nor upon your back and break it. it will be heavy *within* you. like smog. like a dead thing; alive but dying. like how the first breath and the last breath is the same; and in the moment of it, it is difficult to tell which is which.

it will rest upon your bones and tell you that *you are not moving today*. the message comes from a full empty place. a faceless face; nothing seen. and a voiceless voice; nothing heard but it is clear, and it is there. *you are not moving today*. and you will not move. your veins will become hollow like abandoned temples once filled with prayer. not even prayer will move you. and what is prayer if there is no god? and what is atheism if there is one? that thing you were looking forward to suddenly becomes burden, so you will make excuses. *i am not feeling well; i am not feeling myself. i am not feeling.* but then you remember their face and see how it looks at you when you are not there when you said you would be. their face now reminds you of how you feel inside and because you know how it feels to feel this way and you do not want them to feel this way, so you go, to that *thing*. and they, they only feel this way on their face but you, you feel this way in your bones. and it grinds you. all the way to dust. so you go. to that thing. and there you are. moveless. though you thought you beat it, didn't you? at least for today you thought you beat that voice without a voice when you went but it was right when it said *you are not moving today* because you went to this *thing* and you did not move, just like it said. you were there, and you did not move. there are times when you will

move but even in your moving you are moveless, for the times
when you move, and you think you have beaten it by moving you
eventually realise that your moving was on the outside. that even
in the moment of your moving, your inside does not move, and
you feel this. you feel this when your moving is finished, and you
go back to being still. to it being right. that voice without a voice. it
speaks. but for a moment you were happy because they were happy.
for they saw you move but did not know that your moving was not
like theirs though it looked the part.

and you give yourself to your destruction because the fall is much
easier than the climb. the fall is weightless. a perpetual freedom.
the ground is closer to touch than the sky, so why reach up? why
when you will never be able to feel the sky? the sky envelopes. the
sky consumes. it is heavy. and this, this is the root of your afflic-
tion; knowing that you are nothing but this destruction but at
the same time infinitely more than it; knowing that you cannot
escape it - your destruction - for if you do it will push you further
away from them. further on your own. your freedom is liberating.
a weightlessness all of its own but it comes not without pain for
the pain is knowing that you are alone in this. and though your
lonesomeness soothes you it is also your breaking for no one was
born to be alone. too well, you know this. we are born, we die,
and during, we rest in between the tender balance of things. of all
things. though we wish to be we are never quite alone. and though
we wish to be we are never quite included. we exist on the periph-
eries; this tender balance. we carry the degrees of its experience
and it rests heavy in us. on us. of us. it takes too much and gives
too little, yet we feel it all. a heavy weightless thing. if only you
knew that it too breathes. like you. that it's infinite expanding is
like your lungs and the air it breathes is the ethereal star dust of the
universe. it feels and suffers like you. like you it is the bearer of pain
and not just its own. it harbours the pain of those who do not have
their stories told; the silenced; the muted; the forgotten. and that's
why it is heavy on you because you feel their pain; those whose

suffering makes a song in the ears of the deaf and their dancing rythymless feet tramples all over its melody. their pain makes you feel more of your own and so you feel more of theirs. and more of your own. and more of theirs. it is chemical melancholy. and that's why it is beautiful for it does not look at itself with a greater beauty than it looks at others. its shining is not from its own light. if only you knew that you that it is neither your light nor your darkness that scares. it is the beauty of the gentle balance between; this hard softness; this tender strength. that you may find it there. and it, like you, rests in the gentle balance of all things. so, do not just give yourself to one way or too much, to one thing. do not let despair be the heavy upon your soul without hope being the wings that lifts it up. do not stay still.

the missing peace

who's to blame
when a young girl looks in the mirror
and only sees her imperfections?
that she is not the right shape, size or shade
or thin enough to fit into the narrow space
created by society's shrinking minds.
that when she grows up she would have changed
so much of herself that she will become a stranger
to her own childhood eyes. recognise.
who's to blame when boys are taught to validate
their existence through violence or meaningless sex?
neglect their emotions until they become men.
90% perpetrators of all violent crime.

but what do we expect when people feed on lies
and are starved of the truth? where's the proof that we are alive?
that there is a beating heart underneath this burnt flesh.
this burnt flesh that gave birth to the rest. who's to blame
when this knowledge is missing in school
text books or when a child doesn't want to read? look.
education begins when you leave school.
so, read. read. read until it hurts you
and your eyes begin to bleed
because you feel the pain of the words.
the pain of this poetry.

who's to blame when a boy walks hood up
jeans sag low, middle finger to the world?
just because nobody listens. because nobody cares.
who's to blame when that boy is your cousin?
your nephew? your son? who's to blame when that boy was you?
only 10 years ago. that you walk on road
and play Russian roulette with your life

but the only reason you screw up your face and stare
is because you want someone to notice you are alive.

who do you turn to when life gets too much?
when you feel your clutch begin to weaken as you struggle
to hold on? who's to blame when you fall
and no one is there to catch you? when your fears attack you
and depression begins to relax you into an early grave?
we kill ourselves as much as we kill each other
but nobody wants to talk about suicide
because its seen as a weakness. so, we bury these feelings
deep inside and try to mask ourselves but the strongest person
is the one who can admit when they need help.

so, when i call you brother or sister it's not because i'm down
or to try to appear cool, it's because i look at where you are
and i see i've been there too. i've swallowed anger
and spat out rage. felt the fire burn in the pit of my stomach
until i threw up the flames. i used to clench my fists to fight
but now i clench my fists to write.
so, tell me why my fists keep writing?
maybe it's the rage that lives inside me.
maybe it's the peace that's trying to find me.
maybe if we all gave a little piece of ourselves
to each other, we'd be whole again.

man, listen

women belong in two places,
either the bedroom or the kitchen
he said laughing and then looked at me
like i should agree with him.
at that moment i felt sorry for the mother
who raised him and the daughter he may one day have.
i wanted to apologise to every woman in the room
because as the only two guys there our shared gender
did not mean our shared thinking. so i told him
'man, listen,
you've been conditioned
with hyper masculine patriarchal contradictions
like you probably want a woman who is a freak in the sheets
but still a virgin. you want to pay for everything
to assert your masculinity but when a woman doesn't pay you
claim
she's a gold digger. you say women should dress modestly
and not reveal their bodies, but all the pictures you like on Insta-
gram
are the ones that show nudity.
you tell women to act like a lady
but think like a man are you looking for a wife
or one of your bredrins?

man, listen
this isn't your fantasy, this is dangerous thinking.
you've painted a picture of every woman being the same
because there's only one kind you can deal with. ran away
from the ones you could have kept it real with.
so disillusioned by the lies. do you even know
what the real is?

man, listen

i heard your jokes about feminism
but men need feminism too
because men commit suicide
at three times the higher rate than women do.
so, if showing emotions is such a sign of weakness
why does it literally kill us to cry?
why do you say that you are scared
to have a daughter
because you know what men are like?
why not instead raise sons that act right?

man, listen
so, nobody sat down with you
and told you about what being a man means.
and you were raised on commercial hip hop misogyny
Disney and other phony television series and
hollywood movies without anyone to tell you the reality,
well consider that person me.
a man is one when he knows how to be tender
in times of tenderness and strong in times of strength.
it is not about how much you can lift
but how much you can give when there's nothing left.
when your glass heart has been broken into a thousand pieces
how strong will you be to pick up each piece
and love again?

man, listen
this poem isn't for us. it's for our future sons
who deserve not to be raised like us.
the ones who will grow up with hearts that
are numb drowning in shallow lies
because they listen to people like you
who told them how they should feel inside.
and i know it's much more complicated than this.
more than what this poem could accomplish but sometimes i wish
we would just listen.

they only miss you when you're gone

but i miss you
whilst you are still
here. in my presence.
smell your hair
and touch your skin.
hear your voice. kiss your lips
knowing that one day
i will not be able to.

**to those with wings for feet who keep on running
please do not run, fly.**

most days
i spend my days trying to figure out
what the days mean and i'm stuck.
stuck between caring too much and not caring
enough. between holding on too long and letting go
too easily feet stumbling beneath me trying to follow
this narrow path. i look around
and all i see are faces that laugh
grass greener on the other side. eyes wide
brimming smiles. full hearts. music on blast
and the nervous excitement from the accidental
touch of two lovers at the start.
i look at myself and i'm going nowhere. fast.

maybe this is just a façade.
a shallow mask to cover up the fact that
we are all hurting inside.
that no amount of pride could dry
the sea of tears. years of pain.
waiting for clouds to clear. fear
settling like dust. and you know what?
some days i am just tired.
some days i'm barely strong enough
to carry the burden of this heavy heart
let alone the weight of the world on my shoulders.
some days i need some space on my own.
no internet. no mobile phone.
some days i just want to run away from it all.
but then on some days i hear a voice call
in the back of my mind each syllable sounds like
a little droplet of light falling on deaf eyes
that wander through the darkness and it says to me

why would you want to run when you have wings for feet? fly.

so, this is to all those with wings for feet who keep on running
please do not run, fly.

fly like the poets pen off the page.
fly like it was your 12th birthday and you just made
the biggest wish and blew out a candle with a flame
the size of the sun. and the darkness of the universe
is now your living room.

fly like a midnight moonlight city cyclist
with headphones on going downhill
with no hands.

fly
like a runner
in the park racing against the sunset.
no regrets like every mistake you ever made
has just been washed away.

fly like your new crush has just noticed you looking fly
and has walked up to you holding
roses and chocolates to ask you out on a date
and they're paying.

fly like you never stopped believing in love
like you weren't the only one.
there was a time when everything you imagined was real.
your mind is the most powerful instrument you will ever own
only second to your heart which you feel
and they are made of one and the same, so fly.

fly like you are not worried about the days
months and years of getting older
because each day you live is the youngest you will ever be.

we live eternally. in each dream. in each sleep we keep a piece
of ourselves just to give to each other.

so, this is to all those with wings for feet who keep on running
please do not run, fly.

save you

you might need this poem
to lift you up. to remove the heavy
from the sorrows of the world.
to relieve you. to peace together each broken
piece of your soul.
making you whole from everything that keeps
tearing you apart. when you lie sleepless at night
trying to find the reasons to keep up the fight
you might need this poem to remind you
that in the end, everything will be alright.
so, if it's not alright, it's not the end.

i contemplated suicide. until one day i realised
that many already die before they are dead and being
alive does not mean you are living. death begins with
the mind. and too often we already kill ourselves
just from what we think. then the body simply follows
how we feel inside.

you might need this poem to give you hope
when your back is against the ropes.
everything you swallow tastes like lead.
when you choke on air and the voices echo
in your head. when each step feels so heavy.
when each breath feels so heavy.
and you don't know if it's the last one you have left
you might need this poem to remind you that each breath
is the only one you have left
because we can only live in the moment.

our lives are golden but too often
we live in the darkness of our fears
worrying so much about a future that

may never come. my friend died. he was only 32 years.
i remember. on the platform of a train station when we last
spoke he had a light in his eyes as he told me of a new beginning.
who knew so soon that he was going to a different place
where we will all one day go but until then

you might need this poem to save you.

cops and robbers

our kids cannot play
this game, when lying dead on
the floor is practice.

more war

more bombs. air strikes. drones.
more guns. bullets tear bodies.
breaks bones. blood flows
through streets. out homes. more
refugees. families forced to flee.
remember little boy face down
by the sea? and your heavy heart.
what would he say to you now
if he could speak? more
dead women and children.
they have not suffered enough.
'minimise casualties' is okay
as long as it's not one of us. more
ashes to ashes and dreams to dust.
nightmares during sunrise,
it feeds their rush.
their fire. their flame. their heat.
more war, more war, more war,
for more peace.

she is a poem

she is not a poet. she is a poem.
writing herself into the hearts
of everything she touches
but she wouldn't have you know it.
her story is untold
like a flower that never unfolds
to the sun, she has no option but
to search for the light within herself.
her spirit is her wealth
the most precious natural resource
of course, she holds a nation in her palm.
calmed the cries of orphaned babies
and wiped away their tears.
in spite of the suffering and the violence
after all these years
she has vowed never to let go
so with hope she keeps holding on.

you cannot speak to me of being strong
until you have heard the laughter
of a rape survivor caress your spine.
it will paralyse your indifference.
the sunset of her smile
will stay forever in your mind
until that day when you realise
that you are much closer connected
than you think. because when on the brink
of despair everybody stares into the horizon
dreaming of a better day.
if only she could write her own future.
but she isn't a poet, she is a poem
being written into your heart.

something beautiful

something beautiful is happening
right here. right now. in this room.
lifting the gloom from our consciousness
like when the light of the moon
reflects off open water into the night.

something beautiful is happening.
caterpillar to butterfly. rose blossom.
spring bloom. two star crossed lovers' eyes
meet for the first time from across the room.
i dreamed when i was two my grandmother
sat me on her knee and said
*mokili oyo ezali ya yo
na maloba na yo oko komisa yango kitoko.*

and just like you i didn't understand what she said
but the feeling stayed with me
and when i got older i asked my father and he replied
your grandmother talked because she didn't have much time left.
i haven't seen her since
but wherever she is, she stays with me
a woman that i never knew.

on that day
something beautiful happened
when i first wrote poetry. the ground
no longer knew the weight of my feet.
i felt my soul rise eternally. my footprints
were erased from the earth's memory.
i started at infinity and retraced my steps
back to the beginning so i knew both where
i was going and where i had come from.

where i belong, to the constellation of dying stars
whose light does not shine bright enough
for this world to see.
because like the universe i am mostly darkness
and darkness dwells alone
in the corners of dimly lit rooms
or the backs of your mind.
darkness is unknown. undiscovered. unrelenting.

something beautiful is happening
the way our imagination catches fire
when we dream. so, let these words be the match
our breath is the spark
that we may set our future to light
bring it to life from the dark. let us dance
the way that children do.
the way the deaf move to a baseline
they feel only in their soul.
the way my heart beats for you, world.
dream.

it is a declaration to your spirit
that you are alive
and you will never give up.
treat every obstacle like a door
and just walk through it.
place your hands underneath your head
when you sleep at night
so that you may hold on to your dreams.
and never, *never,* let them go.

though i, like you, am filled with fear
and my heart trembles like my hands
but thought they are shaking i dare not let go.

never let go.

know that your being here right now
is by no accident. we will all find our way
back home. but when you arrive leave your fears
at the door and wipe away all of your tears
because we have cried for too long
after all of these years. so, when you return
know that only love is welcome here.

love.

love is something beautiful.
it is the echoes of our beating hearts
in silent solitude and in the stillness. where one day
we will find ourselves.

standing coffin

no one was supposed to die like this.
each day the pain lingers, the debris falls
and the echoing screams grow quieter, as the
few remember, the world forgets.

you walk by carrying your shopping,
drive your car to your weekend getaway
you look up, see a memorium for the dead;
a standing coffin never laid to rest.

Grenfell Tower, 2017

remember me

who will remember us?
the quiet of voice. the soft of heart.
us who would rather part from the path of pain
but would risk it all just to feel again.

who will remember us?
we walk down corridors ignored
as if we are one with the walls.
we are the dreamers
sleepless in our wake
wishing our lives away. the pain
of seeing this world not as it is
but as it should be, lives with us.
in our minds we create
a sanctuary. a solitude. where our souls
are grown kept awake late at night
by our thoughts just so we can go. *to there.*
to find peace
whilst the world sleeps. we
who wear our hearts not on our sleeves
but in our poetry.

in each breath
these words that linger on the edge
of our tongues; words that are never said.
so, we write
because nobody is listening.
nobody hears our silence.
i write because i have nobody to talk to.
walk through each step heavy
like our conscience
the monsters that lurk in the back
of our minds

like fear. rage. love. this is our story.
rip every page out
and spread them across the bed
like rose petals.
stand in your beauty
and show it to your lover.

remember this

the dawn, sunrise
the look of love only seen in their eyes.
moonlight, fireflies and dandelion seeds blowing in the wind.
that every time you see one, you still catch it and make a wish.
that you are someone else's living dream
everyday someone looks at you and thinks
wow
yes, you, *wow*
wow, as you walk past
wow, as you commute on the long ride to work
wow, at your big heart, that keeps on giving
wow at how you make living seem like something that is so easy to
do.
just wow, i want to live this life with you.

you who the gods pray to.
you make the divine look human.
around you, even the most mechanical
hearts feel less mechanical.
and i know the world is heavy
but your tenderness is a gift others wish for.
your breath; look how you've never stopped breathing
through every broken heart, every tragedy
your lungs rise and fall like ocean waves
like rain drops back into the clouds.
like an allergic type ii diabetic eating triple layer chocolate cake,
with gluten, i'd risk it all for you.

you laugh. ah, your laughter. like a chorus, a harmony
of singing voices. have you heard your laugh?
joy tearing sadness at the seams, breaking the dark
cloud of misery, how it bursts, it cracks the sky, the light
of your smile, it shows on your face like a painting. your eyes
a kaleidoscope of two crashing moons, if only you could see

yourself
the way i see you.

bumblebee on petal of flower
butterfly through the meadow.
the stutter of a poet's mouth trying to describe you.
don't give up, tomorrow might be better, i don't know how, it just might
do you remember the last time you gave up?
and yet, here you are, sitting, standing
on the train, reading this, listening, drinking tea
doing things, doing things, doing things
breathing, blood coursing through your veins
heart still beating, still alive; a testimony
that nothing has to be final; you can always try
again, and again, and again.

remember this next time you feel like dying.
next time you feel your world coming to an end.
that among the tragedy, the war, the poverty
the heavy news, tear gas and bombs, the bodies
the floods and the fires, children caged at the border
remember this, that you are loved
that there is infinite goodness in this world
there is beauty; the dawn, sunrise, moonlight, fireflies
a bouquet of dandelions, but most of all, there is you.

.

JJ Bola is a writer, poet, and educator, TEDx Speaker, and UNHCR ambassador.

JJ Bola speaks and performs across London/UK, and internationally, at various institutions, organisations and festivals such SOAS, Oxford, Kings, Glastonbury Festival, Cheltenham Literature Festival, World Economic Forum (Devos), Goethe Institut Lagos, and more. His work is featured across a number of platforms and publications such as the BBC, the Guardian, Media Diversified, Electric Literature, Mechanics Institute Review and the Wellcome Collection.

JJ Bola is represented by Pontas Literary & Film agency. He lives in London

NO PLACE TO CALL HOME
by JJ Bola

"Deep inside each and every one of us, we are all always reaching for a place we can call home"

JJ Bola's debut novel *No Place To Call Home* was published by OWN IT! in hardback and eBook to critical aclaim in 2017. It is now also available in paperback.

With colourful characters and luminous prose, *No Place To Call Home* is a tale of belonging, identity and immigration, of hope and hopelessness, of loss - not by death, but by distance - and by no means the least, of love.

WWW.OWNIT.LONDON
@OWNITLDN